for Lewis & Faye

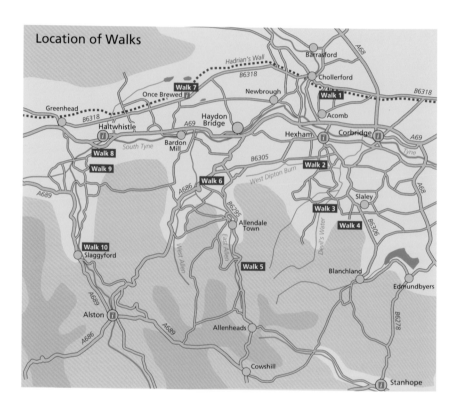

Location of Walks

Barrasford · A68
Hadrian's Wall · Chollerford
B6318
Once Brewed 🖷 · **Walk 7** · Newbrough · **Walk 1** · B6318
Greenhead · B6318 · Acomb
Haltwhistle 🖷 · A69 · Haydon Bridge · Hexham 🖷 · Corbridge 🖷 · A69
South Tyne · Bardon Mill · Tyne
Walk 8 · B6305
Walk 9 · West Dipton Burn · **Walk 2**
A689 · A686 · **Walk 6** · Slaley
B6295 · **Walk 3**
Allendale Town · **Walk 4** · B6306
Walk 10 · West Allen · East Allen · Devil's Water
Slaggyford · **Walk 5** · Blanchland
Edmundbyers
A689 · Alston 🖷 · B6278
A686 · A689 · Allenheads
Cowshill
Stanhope 🖷

Contents

Introduction

South-west Northumberland is probably best known for the impressive remains of Hadrian's Wall that straddle the high cliffs of the Whin Sill escarpment and are still a potent reminder of a long-lost empire. The upland landscapes that provide the setting for the Wall give meaning to the description of Northumberland as 'the land of the far horizon' and convey a very tangible sense of the wilderness and tranquillity for which the area is renowned. To the south of the Wall, the South Tyne and Allen valleys are perhaps a little less spectacular but they have a very special character and charm which owe much to their distinctive cultural and historic heritage. Along this northern edge of the North Pennines there are rivers, woods, farms and moors that are riddled with footpaths and bridleways, with a smattering of pleasant village pubs for the thirsty walker. The geology of this area is especially fascinating with rich veins of ore that for centuries have been mined for lead, silver, copper, iron, fluospar and other minerals. This industrial past is etched into the landscape and culture of the valleys and can be seen in the remains of former mine workers' cottages and old Methodist chapels and along the pack horse trails that were used to carry the ore and metal ingots over the moors to Tyneside.

This book describes ten circular walks that offer you the opportunity to explore and enjoy this fascinating and beautiful part of Northumberland. The routes vary in length from about 4 to 6 miles and take in a variety of different landscapes, from the hills and moors above Slaley (Walk 4) and along Hadrian's Wall (Walk 7) to the riverside woodlands near Featherstone (Walk 9) and Hexham (Walk 2) and the remoter valleys of the North Pennines at Spartylea (Walk 5) and Slaggyford (Walk 10). These walks have been chosen to show you some of the most attractive and interesting parts of south west Northumberland and it is hoped that the interpretive notes will help you to enjoy and learn about the natural, cultural and historic heritage of this area and to understand the human and natural forces that have shaped the landscape we see today. Should you wish to buy some refreshments during your day out, the introduction to each walk gives the location of nearby restaurants and cafés 🍽, pubs 🍺 and shops 🛍 which we hope you will support during your visit.

Walk Routes

The book is aimed at anyone who wants to spend a few hours enjoying a pleasant and interesting walk with the opportunity for a pub lunch, afternoon tea or an ice cream to finish off. At the start of each walk there is a brief introduction to give you a flavour of the route that you will take. This is followed by a note of the 1:25000 OS Explorer Map for the walk and the six figure grid reference for the start; an indication of its degree of difficulty (easy, moderate or strenuous); its length and the time that it should take to complete (allowing for a few stops along the way); and the height and gradient of any uphill sections. To help you get the most out of your walk and learn something about the area's history, culture and wildlife, lots of information is included about points of interest along the way.

The walks mostly follow designated public footpaths and bridleways: these are normally signposted (with timber finger posts) only where they leave a public highway. Waymarkers may have been installed at other locations (e.g. on a stile or at a gateway) where the alignment of a right of way is unclear. In some cases the walks cross 'access land' where you have a 'right to roam' (see below for details). On a couple of occasions the walk route has been provided by the landowner or is used with their consent: in these cases the routes are marked on the maps as 'permissive access' (see page 6 for map key).

Access Land and the 'Right to Roam'

Much of the open hill land in south west Northumberland is defined as 'access land' (under the terms of the Countryside and Rights of Way Act 2000) where the public has a 'right to roam' wherever they want – but only on foot, not by cycle or on a horse. These areas are clearly signed at both entry and exit points (see examples below) and are also shown on the new editions of the Ordnance Survey 'Explorer Maps' (1: 25000) although it is important to be aware that restrictions to this right of access may apply at certain times of year or in certain locations: so please be sure to comply with any notices that may have been posted.

Access Land

End of Access Land

Maps

The start point for each of the ten walks is shown on the location map on page 2. The individual maps for each walk have been drawn specially for this book and are carefully cross referenced to the route descriptions in the text with the aim of making it as simple as possible for you to find your way. Alongside information about the nature of the route, reference is made to different structures such as gates, stiles, finger posts and waymarkers that you will encounter along the way. The walks in this book are covered by the following OS maps:

- 1:25000 Explorer Map OL43 (Hadrian's Wall): Walks 1, 2, 3, 4, 5 (part), 6, 7, 8, 9 & 10
- 1:25000 Explorer Map OL31 (North Pennines): Walk 5 (part)

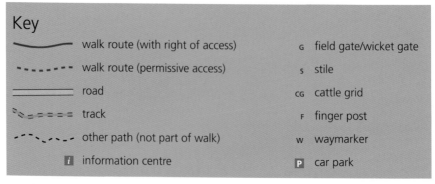

Key

———— walk route (with right of access)	G	field gate/wicket gate
- - - - - - - walk route (permissive access)	S	stile
════════ road	CG	cattle grid
⸗⸗⸗⸗⸗⸗ track	F	finger post
-⸗⸗⸗⸗⸗- other path (not part of walk)	W	waymarker
🛈 information centre	P	car park

Looking after the Countryside

Most of the land along these walks is privately owned. It is in everyone's interest to look after the countryside and to leave it as they would like to find it. In particular, fasten all gates and keep to the recognised route, especially when crossing enclosed farmland. It is also important to act responsibly and considerately by keeping to the Country Code - so take any litter home, don't disturb livestock and, if you wish to take a dog, keep it on a lead at all times.

Safety Advice

All of these walks are along paths and tracks across open countryside and there are a number of points that should be borne in mind, especially if you are taking young children.

Weather & Clothing

Comfort is essential to the enjoyment of any walk so wear comfortable, sensible shoes or boots. From May to October conditions underfoot will usually be fairly good, although at other times of the year or after heavy rain the ground may be soft and boggy in places. Walking can also be warm work but, especially at higher levels, it is possible to become chilled so take an extra layer of clothing just in case the temperature drops.

Even in summer rain clouds can sweep in remarkably quickly and, in the best traditions of the British climate, what promises to be a warm, clear and sunny day can soon turn out to be cool, wet and windy. So, however good the weather forecast always take a waterproof, remembering that it can keep out the wind as well as the rain.

Hopefully you will experience none of these more capricious elements of the weather and you will enjoy your walk on a fine day with blue skies. At such times the sun can be strong and you can get thirsty - so go prepared with a hat, sun cream and plenty to drink.

Hazards

Some of the walks include steep ascents and descents: these may be grassy, rocky or have a loose stony surface. Take great care, especially if the ground is wet and slippery, remembering that more accidents happen going downhill than uphill. On Walk 2, the public footpath along the West Dipton Burn includes a difficult section over some stream-side rocks which should be avoided if you are not fit and sure-footed or if the water level in the Burn is too high: if in doubt, turn back (see route description for more information).

Some walks also include sections along minor roads. Although many of these roads are likely to be relatively quiet, walkers should, wherever possible, use the pavement or verge. If you have to walk on the road, keep to the right hand side so that you face oncoming vehicles and be sure to watch and listen for approaching traffic.

Mobile Phones

A mobile phone can save your life in an emergency but remember that out of towns coverage can be patchy and you may not be able to get through - so don't rely on your mobile to get you out of trouble.

1. Heavenfield and Fallowfield Dene

STARTING AT THE SITE OF A MEDIAEVAL BATTLE, this walk follows the line of Hadrian's Wall before heading south across farmland to Fallowfield Dene, a lovely wooded valley which once lay at the heart of a thriving mining industry. The return leg starts out along quiet country lanes before crossing Fallowfield Fell where you can still see the quarries excavated 2000 years ago by the Roman army to provide building stone for the Wall.

OS Map: *1:25000 Explorer Map OL43 (Hadrian's Wall)*
Start: *NY 937694*
Grade: *Fairly easy*
Length: *3.9 miles (6.3 km) and about 2½ hours*
Ascent: *120 metres (400 feet) on gentle gradients*

Local services 🚍 Heavenfield, Hexham, Chollerford

🚌 Hexham, Chollerford, Wall, Acomb, Anick, Stagshaw

🚉 Hexham

Park in the 'Heavenfield' lay-by which is situated on the north side of the B6318 about 1 mile to the east of Chollerford.

From the west end of the layby, go through a gate close to a large wooden cross. Our walk heads diagonally left across the field and then alongside a dry stone wall but, before starting, it is worth visiting Heavenfield Church which was built close to where Saint Oswald is believed to have erected a cross and prayed to God before the Battle of Heavenfield in 635AD (see Box A).

Back on the route of the walk, head west along the grass path which soon crosses a stile to pass through an area of woodland and then along the edge of open fields.

Barley fields at Fallowfield Far

1 At the corner of the field the path comes to a stile close to the junction between a tarmac track and the main road. Go over the stile, turn left to cross the road (taking great care to watch and listen for oncoming traffic) then down a few steps into a field. The route of our walk goes straight ahead across the field along the path signed 'Public Footpath: Fallowfield 1', but take a few moments to have a look at the remains of Hadrian's Wall over to your right. (see Box B).

A The Battle of Heavenfield was fought in about 635AD between a Northumbrian army under Oswald and the Welsh army of King Cadwallon. A couple of years previously, Cadwallon had defeated the Northumbrian King Edwin and killed his two successors, prompting Oswald to return from years of exile to claim the Northumbrian throne.

In 635 Cadwallon and his English ally, King Penda of Mercia (present day Midlands), marched from York and met Oswald's army here, just north of Hexham. Oswald took up a defensive position so that his army faced east with its flanks protected to the north by Brady's Crag and to the south by Hadrian's Wall (which would have run east/west across the field between the church and the road). According to Bede, Oswald raised a cross and prayed for victory alongside his troops.

Although the Welsh had superior numbers, they were forced to attack along a narrow front and were eventually defeated. The remnants of the army fled south with many of the Welsh soldiers, including Cadwallon, being killed. The battle was a decisive victory for Oswald and, as king of Northumbria, he is credited by Bede with restoring Christianity to the region. Oswald was only to spend eight years on the throne before being killed by King Penda at the Battle of Maserfield in Shropshire.

Heavenfield Church in late autumn

2 Go over a stile in a fence and turn sharp left along the edge of the field. At the top of the field climb over another stile and turn half right to a gate beside a narrow country road. Go across the road, over a pair of stiles and walk up the hill straight ahead (signed 'Public Footpath: Fallowfield ¾'). At the top of the hill bear right to a field gate then (following the route of the electricity line) through another gate and across a pasture field. This brings you to yet another gate and onto the driveway for Crag House where you should turn left, to go between the stone gateposts and onto the minor road above Fallowfield Farm.

B This short surviving section of Hadrian's Wall gives just a hint of what it might have looked like when it was first built in about 125 AD, 'to separate the Romans from the barbarians'. The Wall stretched for 74 miles from Wallsend, near Newcastle, to Bowness on the Cumbrian coast and is believed to have been about 15 Roman feet (4.4 metres) high and 2 - 3 metres thick. It took about 15 years to build and for almost 300 years it protected Rome's northern frontier in Britain, except for a brief interlude between about 140AD and 160AD when this was frontier moved to the new Antonine Wall between the Forth and the Clyde.

Thirteen forts were built along its length, each about a day's march apart with milecastles evenly spaced at intervals of one Roman mile (about 0.9 of a modern mile). The remains of Housesteads Fort lie close to the B6318 about 10 miles to the west of here and are well worth a visit if you have time.

Immediately to the north of the Wall the Romans constructed a defensive ditch about three metres deep and eight metres wide - the remains of this are still visible as a shallow depression. To the south of the wall there was a ditch with banks to either side called a 'Vallum' which served to delineate the southern edge of the military zone around the Wall; this can also still be seen as you continue your walk across the field.

3 Turn right down the road to Fallowfield Farm. Immediately before the first farm buildings on the left side of the road, turn left along the track signed 'Public Bridleway: Salmonswell 1½'.

4 Just past the gate below Square Wood, the track forks: here, keep left to follow a grass track across a field. At the wall on the far side of the field, go through a gate and bear right down towards Fallowfield Dene.

Fallowfield Dene

5 About 50 metres through the gate into Fallowfield Dene, the path comes to a T-junction: turn left and follow the woodland path heading upstream beside the Red Burn. This path takes you over two footbridges and eventually brings you to a road close to Codlaw Dene Farm. In past centuries this area was extensively mined for coal and iron ore and there are still many dangerous old bell-pits, ventilation shafts and mining tunnels, so keep to the path and do not go near any of the old workings - and if you have a dog, please keep it on a lead.

6 Turn left up the road past Codlaw Dene Farm. This is usually a quiet road but you should still take care to watch and listen for oncoming traffic, especially around the double bend at the top of the hill. At Codlaw Hill, keep left (signed 'Chollerford 2½') to follow the road past Fir Trees.

C The woodlands along Fallowfield Dene are littered with the remains of the mining activity that took place here during the 18th and 19th centuries. Some of the pits and shafts are in a dangerous condition so keep to the path and do not go near any of the old workings – and if you have a dog, please keep it on a lead.

The mines here were some of the most productive in this part of the Tyne Valley and were worked for lead, coal, iron and witherite, a barium carbonate mineral. Witherite is extremely rare and was mined in only a few places across the globe. Its main commercial use was in the production of glass, bricks and cement and in the manufacture of Josiah Wedgwood's famous 'Jasper ware'. It is also highly poisonous and took a heavy toll on the health of the Fallowfield miners. For the same reason, people living close to the old witherite mines had to be careful to thoroughly wash their home-grown vegetables.....and local cats that consumed the mineral by licking their paws tended not to live too long.

7 About 200 metres past Fir Trees turn left through a large gate (signed 'Public Footpath: Fallowfield 1¼ Fallowfield Fell ¾') and head straight across the field to a gateway in a stone wall. Through the gate, continue in the same direction across the next field to a stile in a stone wall that takes you onto the moorland of Fallowfield Fell.

8 About 80 metres beyond the stile there is a waymarker post: here turn right to cross a stile in a fence and then follow a grass path that curves to the left uphill past two more waymarker posts. Over the brow of the hill, the path heads slightly right (and slightly uphill) across the Fell.

9 Through two gates you will come to a road: here, turn right. This takes you back to the start, but take great care crossing the main road because, although visibility is good, traffic can travel at speed. If you feel like some refreshment, St Oswald's Tearooms are about ¼ mile to the east: you can drive or, if you are still feeling energetic, you can walk along the Hadrian's Wall Path (back through the gate beside the cross and along the grass path to the right).

D The construction of Hadrian's Wall, with all of its associated forts, milecastles, roads and earthworks, was a massive undertaking, even for the Roman army, and it is thought that it took about 15 years to complete. The outer faces of the Wall were built from roughly dressed sandstone which retained a core of rubble bonded with clay or mortar. All of this stone had to be obtained locally and the Roman quarry at Written Crag is just one of many that are scattered along the length of the Wall. The legionaries did most of the construction work themselves, with each legion containing skilled builders, architect-engineers, surveyors, stone masons, carpenters and glaziers, while the soldiers themselves tended to specialise in the construction of forts and other military buildings.

Written Crag is so named because in the early 19th century a stone was found with the Roman inscription PETRA FLAVI CARANTINI, possibly carved by the foreman of a gang working at the quarry or, if you are of a romantic nature, maybe by a local girl who was in love with him. Unfortunately, the stone was badly defaced and some years ago it was removed for safe keeping and can now be seen at Chesters Museum.

The old Roman quarry at Written Crag and a 19th century line drawing of the inscribed stone when it was still in its original location

2. Dipton Mill, Dotland and Letah Wood

THE BEST TIME TO DO THIS WALK IS IN EARLY APRIL when the banks of wild daffodils in Letah Wood are in full bloom and spring is on its way. At any other time of year you will still enjoy a pleasant stroll along streamside paths and through the fields and woods of 'Hexhamshire'. This walk is quite strenuous and in places can be heavy and muddy after bad weather but, as a reward for your efforts, when you get to the end you will find a pleasant country pub serving lunches and locally brewed ales. Before you start, please read the 'Note' below.

OS Map: *1:25000 Explorer Map OL43 (Hadrian's Wall)*
Start: *NY930610*
Grade: *Strenuous, with one short but tricky section along the West Dipton Burn*
Length: *6.4 miles (10.3 km) and about 4 hours*
Ascent: *150 metres (490 feet) on gentle gradients*

Local services   ☕   Hexham

☉   Dipton Mill, Hexham, Slaley

🕯   Hexham

From Hexham, take the B6308 to Slaley and Blanchland. After ¼ mile bear right along Dipton Mill Road and follow this for a further 1½ miles to the bottom of a long hill, where you should park in the open area on the left side of the road, opposite the Dipton Mill Inn.

Note: The first 500 metres of public footpath through West Dipton Wood can be boggy especially after wet weather, but don't be put off, it soon gets better. Also, please be aware that there is a short but difficult section of stream-side path along the West Dipton Burn (see ❶ below) which should be avoided if you are not fit and sure-footed or if the water level in the burn is too high: if in doubt, you should consider turning back.

Walk back across the bridge over the West Dipton Burn and turn left over a stile along the footpath signed 'Public Footpath: West Dipton Wood'.

Black Hall

1 After about 200 metres, just over a small stream, take the path to the right which takes you uphill around a loop in the Burn before dropping back down to continue along the valley bottom. Close to Rot Sike the public footpath follows a rocky path along the edge of the stream. Please take great care on this section because it is often wet and slippery and should definitely not be attempted if the water level is high. If in any doubt, regrettably you may be best to consider turning back and doing a different walk.

A Besides being one of the prettiest parts of Tynedale, the woodlands along the West Dipton Burn also have an important place in English history. In 1464 the Wars of the Roses had been going on for 9 years and showed little sign of an early resolution. The Battle of Hexham, fought on 15 May that year, was just one of a series of bloody exchanges between the Houses of Lancaster and York and ended in the defeat of the Lancastrian force under the command of the Duke of Somerset. Whilst Somerset was beheaded in Hexham market place shortly after the battle, his king, Henry VI, was safely tucked away in Bywell Castle a few miles to the east. Meanwhile, legend has it, Henry's Queen, Margaret of Anjou, had tagged along with the Lancastrian soldiers to give them moral support and, after the defeat, is believed to have fled the battlefield to seek shelter in Dipton Wood where she bartered her jewels to save the lives of herself and her son, Prince Edward. A damp cavern about 2.5km to the west of Dipton Mill is still called the 'Queen's Cave'.

The West Dipton Burn in sprin...

2 Go left across the concrete footbridge over the Burn and head uphill along a rocky path through the wood and then between open fields. On reaching the road, continue straight ahead.

3 At the crossroads, go across the main road (taking care to watch and listen for traffic) and turn right over a stile beside a gate (signed 'Public Footpath: Dotland ¾') to head uphill across a field. Over the brow of the ridge, make for a stile in the fence ahead and continue through the next field, with a tumbled-down stone wall and an old hedge to your right. Over the stile in the top corner, the path heads for the left-hand end of the buildings at Dotland, with the line being indicated by the waymarker arrow on the stile: if this field has been sown with an arable crop, the route is usually marked out.

4 Climb a stile beside a gate and turn left along the roadside verge. 50 metres further on turn left again over another stile (signed 'Public Footpath: Whitley Mill 1') then, after going over two more stiles, make for the gates at the left-hand corner of the wood around Dotland Grange. Continuing in the same direction, walk along the left side of the wood then through some pasture fields.

B The Ordnance Survey map of the area shows the site of a 'Mediaeval Village' just to the south east of Dotland. As you cross the stile over the roadside wall you will be able to pick out the humps and hollows of the cottages and garden walls that once formed part of the largest settlement between Hexham and the moors of the North Pennines to the south. Like many towns and villages in England, Dotland was devasted by the bubonic plague, or 'Black Death', that swept across Europe in the middle of the 14th century. By the late 17th century, records show that Dotland had recovered to about 20 households, with a village green and well and was surrounded by open fields and common land. As you continue your walk over the next stile, you will cross a pasture field with the characteristic pattern of 'rigg and furrow' which probably dates from this time and would have been created by ploughing the land with a simple fixed plough pulled by a team of oxen.

Over the decades that followed, the population once again went into decline as traditional farming patterns were swept away by the Enclosure Acts and young men were able to find employment in the growing coal and lead mining industries of Tyneside and the North Pennines. In the end Dotland probably just declined until there was no-one left, rather than being abandoned through some collective exodus or as a result of some catastrophic event.

5 At the end of a line of old hawthorn bushes and, just after passing under an electricity line, you will come to a steep gorse covered bank above the Ham Burn. From here, turn left across the field to a large electricity pole with two cross-pieces (where the electricity lines meet) and then past the right-hand end of a small group of old ash trees. At this point, bear slightly left to cross a stream at the left-hand end of a wood, then slightly right to make for the mid-point of an old stone wall around a narrow plantation of beech trees.

6 Climb over a broken-down section of the plantation wall then over a stone step stile on the far side: here, a waymarker arrow on a post directs you over the summit of a knoll in the field ahead. From the knoll, make your way across the fields then along a walled track to the hamlet of Black Hall.

7 Go through Black Hall and down the tarmac driveway. Close to the end of a belt of trees on your left, turn left over two stiles (the first is a stone step-stile) and head up a field, keeping a stone wall close by on your right. (A small log half way up offers a good spot for a rest and picnic.). Continue through the eastern end of Black Hall Wood then along the edge of two fields to the farm at Smelting Syke: here, follow the waymarkers through two gates to reach a road.

[C] Many of the trees, shrubs and stone walls alongside this country lane are covered in patches of lichen, with the most striking being the yellow/orange *Xanthoria parietina* or 'golden shield lichen' which seems to have a particular preference for the branches of old elder bushes. One such bush grows very close to the stile over the roadside wall on the path towards Dotland Park.

Lichens are strange organisms in which a fungus and an alga grow together, with each benefiting from the presence of the other. The algal cells, through the process of photosynthesis, provide the fungus with organic nutrients whilst, in return, the water, minerals and gases absorbed from the environment by the fungus are shared with the algae. *Xanthoria parietina* is quite common in farming areas because its thrives on the high levels of nitrogen in the atmospheric dust, for example from fertilisers, manure and slurry, and livestock. For the same reason, it is also common on coastal cliffs close to seabird colonies. Medieval healers took the colour of this lichen as a sign that it was a cure for jaundice: not surprisingly, it isn't.

8 Turn left and walk along the roadside verge. After about 150 metres go right over a ladder stile (signed 'Public Footpath: Dotland Park ½') and, following the direction indicated by the sign finger-board, head across a small stream and over Cockshaw Rigg to a gate in the far field corner. Through the gate, follow the track through several more gates to skirt around the left side of the farm buildings at Dotland Park. In front of the house, bear left along the tarmac driveway: this leads to a junction with Hill Road.

9 At Hill Road, you have two choices: you can go straight across and down the track back to the start; or you can turn right along the road to visit Letah Wood – a 'must' in April when the wild daffodils are out. To get there, follow the road for about ½ mile, taking care to watch and listen for oncoming traffic. Just past Newbiggin Hill there is a stile over the fence on the left (signed 'Public Footpath: Dipton Mill ¾ Hexham 2¼') - this is your route back to the pub. 150 metres further along the road there is a small Woodland Trust sign and map on the right. Close by, there are steps down into the wood but, be very careful, the paths through the wood are quite rough and you will need to find your way across the Letah Burn and along some eroded river banks. (For more information, see Box D on Page 20)

10 To return to Dipton Mill, go over the stile near Newbiggin Hill and head for a gate in the bottom left corner of the field (the line of the path is indicated by the finger-board of the sign). Climb over a stile beside the gate and follow the path alongside the West Dipton Burn. At the end of the field, cross the footbridge and continue upstream on the right-hand bank of the burn. On reaching the road, turn left back to the car park.

Woodlands along the West Dipton Burn

D From the road near Newbiggin Hill you get a good view of Letah Wood, a Woodland Trust property that is renowned for its show of native wild daffodils (*Narcissus pseudonarcissus*) which are at their best in early April; a few weeks later than the cultivated varieties that you will have in your garden. If you want to explore Letah Wood, there is a network of rough and informal paths but these can be difficult to negotiate due to fallen trees, eroding river banks, steep slopes and the need to cross streams without the aid of a footbridge - so, if you go into the wood, do take great care!

Wild daffodils now survive in just a few places in the British Isles, with many colonies having been lost over the last two centuries as people dug up the bulbs to plant in their gardens or to sell. The Woodland Trust acquired Letah Wood in the 1990s to protect the whole woodland ecosystem – including the daffodils - which probably has very ancient origins dating back many thousands of years.

3. Dukesfield and the Devil's Water

A COUPLE OF CENTURIES AGO Dukesfield was a thriving industrial centre where ore, carried by pack horse from the mines of the North Pennines, was smelted to produce lead ingots which were then transported to the four corners of the British Empire. Nowadays there are few traces of its industrial past but this pleasant walk along the valley of the Devil's Water will help you to explore and understand some of the area's history and to enjoy the wildlife and landscape of this beautiful part of Hexhamshire.

OS Map: *1:25000 Explorer Map OL43 (Hadrian's Wall)*
Start: *NY943581*
Grade: *Moderate, with few hills and mostly on well-surfaced tracks and paths*
Length: *4.2 miles (6.7 km) and about 2½ hours*
Ascent: *95 metres (310 feet) on gentle gradients*

Local services ☕ Hexham & Slaley
 🍺 Dipton Mill, Hexham & Slaley
 🛒 Hexham & Slaley

From the centre of Hexham, take the B6309 heading south to Slaley and Blanchland (at this junction reset the trip on your milometer – the parking place for the start of the walk is 4.8 miles from here). After ¼ mile take the right fork along the Dipton Mill Road, signed to Whitley Chapel, Dye House and Juniper, then after another ¼ mile, turn left for Dye House, Juniper and Ordley. After a couple more miles, go through the village of Juniper, then across the bridge over the Rowley Burn to the hamlet of Steel. At the T-junction just past Steel, turn left (signed to Slaley and Blanchland) down to the bridge over the Devil's Water. On the far side of the bridge (at 4.8 miles), park in the rough lay-by on the right-hand side of the road, taking care not to block the gateway.

Go through a gate at the bottom of the layby (signed 'Public Footpath' on the opposite side of the road) and follow a stone track heading upstream along the Devil's Water.

1 Go through a gate and continue along the track through a meadow.

2 At the gate just past Redlead Mill, turn right to cross a footbridge over the Devil's Water. On the far side of the bridge, turn sharp left to follow an attractive woodland path that continues upstream.

Hexhamshire

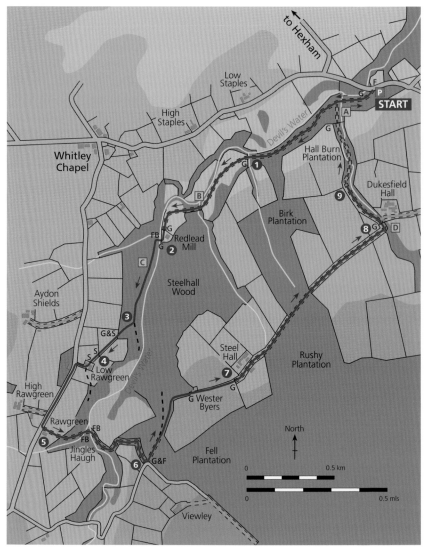

3 At the fork in the path, keep right to go uphill towards a gate in the stone wall along the edge of the wood. Climb over a stile beside the gate and head left towards Low Rawgreen, keeping a stone wall and then a fence close by on your left.

4 At Low Rawgreen, follow the driveway between the cottages then around to the right to reach a road: here, turn left to walk along the roadside verge, taking care to watch and listen for oncoming traffic.

A According to the 'Blackgate Deed', smelting of lead ore took place at Dukesfield as long ago as 1588. The two stone arches to the left of the track are all that remain of the Dukesfield Mill which, during the 18th and 19th centuries, smelted lead ore extracted from the lead mines of Weardale and Allendale. The mill itself lay over to your right on the other side of the track but its six furnaces have disappeared completely: these arches supported the flue which carried the poisonous fumes from the mill to four chimneys located further up the valley side. The Dukesfield Mill was one of the largest in the North Pennines and, at its peak late in the 18th century, it smelted over 3200 tons (3.25m kilos) of lead ore a year. The mill was eventually demolished in 1837 with much of the stone being used to build barns and byres at nearby Dukesfield Hall, which you will pass later in your walk.

B Many of the trees that grow along the banks of the Devil's Water are common alder (*Alnus glutinosa*). Across the world there are about 30 different species of alder growing as far afield as Alaska, Peru and China but the common alder is the only species that is native to the British Isles. It is well adapted to damp streamside habitats where it can grow along the water's edge. The seeds have minute air bags on either side which keep them afloat as they drift downstream until they are washed up on the bankside and are able to germinate and grow into a new tree.

Alder timber has little commercial value although it was once commonly used to produce some of the finest charcoal which, along with sulphur and saltpetre, were used in the manufacture of gunpowder. Going even further back in time, the Romans found that the trunks are very resistant to wet rot and, once hollowed out, made excellent water pipes.

[C] The mounds of pine needles, leaves and twigs alongside the path have been built by colonies of wood ants which, on warm days, can be seen scurrying around in their thousands foraging for food or collecting minute pieces of forest litter to add to the pile. They are becoming quite rare in Northumberland so please do not disturb the nests.

Wood ant colonies are usually found on the edge of conifer plantations where there is light and a good food supply and the sun can provide adequate warmth. Each colony can support as many as 100,000 ants and is like a little town, with living accommodation, nurseries, food stores, road links and even cemeteries for dead ants. Ants are essentially predators and feed mainly on other insects such as caterpillars, and beetles. When they leave the nest to look for food they leave a scent track behind them so that they do not get lost and others can follow. Long established colonies may have foraging trails extending as far as 30 metres from the nest and some will climb up nearby trees where there is often abundant prey hiding amongst the nooks and crannies in the bark. The photograph above left shows a wood ant feeding on the honeydew, a sugary liquid secreted by aphids.

5 At Rawgreen, turn left down a stone track which soon drops down to the Devil's Water. Go over the two footbridges at Jingles Haugh and bear right along a rough track that runs alongside the river, then heads left to wind its way up the valley side. (Jingles Haugh gets its name from the sound made by the bells on the teams of pack horses that once used to cross the stream here on their way to Dukesfield Mill, carrying lead from the mines in the North Pennines).

6 At the junction with a tarmac road, turn left through a gate (signed 'Public Bridleway') and walk along a woodland track towards Wester Byers. After 200 metres be sure to take the right fork to keep to the path along the woodland edge. Past the old stone barn at Wester Byers, walk along the edge of a field, keeping a stone wall close by on your left.

7 Approaching Steel Hall, you will go through a gate and onto a stone track that takes you past the farm buildings and then on to Dukesfield Hall.

8 Close to Dukesfield Hall the track takes a sharp turn left then goes through a gate (often left open). As the track then bends to the right, turn left along a slightly narrower track between a high hedge and the woodlands that surround the Hall (before doing so, it is worth continuing the few metres to have a look at the buildings of Dukesfield Hall – see Box D)

9 Just past a field gate on the left, the track bears slightly right into Hall Burn Plantation - this is a permissive path which you can use by kind permission of the Allendale Estates. Ignoring the side-tracks first to the right and then to the left, continue down to the bottom of the wood, then past a barrier to reach the track that you followed on the outward leg of the walk: here, turn right to get back to the start.

D Dukesfield Hall has a fascinating history that is very closely tied into the Dukesfield Mill, the remains of which you saw earlier on your walk. The Hall was once the residence of the manager of the Mill and, close by, you can still see the old stone 'bothy' (see photograph below) which was a way-station for the packhorse trains that brought lead ore from Allendale to the smelt mill. The horses were kept on the ground floor, while the drivers, or 'jaggers' as they were known, slept on the first floor where they were kept warm by the heat rising from the animals below. The presence of a dovecot in the roof - still in use centuries later - would have been no accident, with its residents finding their way into many a pigeon pie to feed the hungry jaggers.

From the Dukesfield Mill the lead ingots were carried by packhorse along the 'Lead Road' to Blaydon on the River Tyne, from where they would have been transported across the world. On their return journey from Blaydon, the packhorse trains picked up coal from the collieries at Kiln Pit Hill and brought it to Dukesfield to fire the furnaces. On the last leg back to Allendale, they probably carried food, salt or other goods that could be sold to the North Pennine mining communities.

4. Across Blanchland Moor

THIS IS ONE OF MY FAVOURITE WALKS IN NORTHUMBERLAND and, whilst it is quite long, it is an easy route with few hills and good conditions underfoot for most of the way. The route takes you across some open and exposed moorlands so pick a fine day with clear skies and gentle breezes: August is a good month, when you will see the heather at its best. From Blanchland Moor there are stunning views in all directions but especially to the west over the valley of the Devil's Water. Afterwards, you will understand why the uplands of Northumberland are called 'the land of the far horizon'.

OS Map: *1:25000 Explorer Map OL43 (Hadrian's Wall)*
Start: *NY955552*
Grade: *Moderate, with few hills and mostly on well-surfaced tracks and paths*
Length: *6.7 miles (10.8 km) and about 4½ hours*
Ascent: *105 metres (345 feet) on gentle gradients*

Local services   Hexham, Slaley & Blanchland
   Slaley, Dipton Mill & Hexham
   Hexham, Slaley & Blanchland

From Hexham, take the B6308 to Slaley and Blanchland. Close to Slaley, and about ½ mile past the Travellers Rest pub, turn right onto the minor road heading south, signed to 'Ladycross'. Drive along here for 2 miles and at the end of the tarmac road, park on the edge of the stone-surfaced parking area, taking care not to block any of the access tracks.

From the parking area walk straight ahead along the track signed 'Public Byway'. Follow this track for about 500 metres, ignoring any side-tracks to left and right: this takes you to the forest edge at Actoncleugh Head.

Heather moorland on Acton Fell, with Slaley Forest in the distance

1 Go through the gate and keep straight ahead along the track heading across the moor. After 100 metres be sure to take the left fork to continue along the main moorland track (the right fork takes you back into the forest): follow this across Blanchland Moor, passing through two gates along the way, until you come to Pennypie House.

2 Close to the entrance gate to Pennypie House, bear right to cross the footbridge over the Shildon Burn and continue along the track (signed 'Baybridge').

A These upland heather moors of the North Pennines are managed primarily for grouse shooting, with the season starting each year on the 'glorious' 12th August and running through until December 10th. To the right of the path you will see a row of circular stone grouse butts which, on a shooting day, will be occupied by the 'guns'. Each section of moor will be shot about eight times during the season and, whatever one's feelings about the shooting of game-birds, there is no doubt that it is vitally important to the economy of these upland areas, providing much needed employment for local communities and generating significant income for the estates.

A well managed moor such as this will support a good population of grouse and, as you walk along, you may well see them break cover and fly off at low level, emitting their characteristic barking call which sounds like 'go-bak, go-bak-bak-bak-bak.' It is their habit of flying low and fast that makes grouse so tricky to shoot and hence so popular as a quarry. The aim of management is to use a rotational program of burning to create a mosaic of different ages of heather, with the young heather providing a nutritious food supply whilst the older heather is best for nesting and offers cover from inclement weather and predators. Each winter small patches of old heather are burnt off, with the heather regenerating the following spring from the burnt stumps or from heather seed stored in the soil. Some of these burnt patches can be seen scattered across this hillside.

Shooting butts and a red grouse on Bulbeck Common

B Bulbeck Moor gets its name from the Barony of Bolbec, which was bestowed on Hugue de Bolbec by William the Conqueror as a reward for his family's support during the Duke's successful invasion of England in 1066. It is said that Hugue's brother, Gautier Giffard, not only provided William with ships and men for his invasion but also gave him the horse that he rode during the Battle of Hastings.

After the invasion William was extremely generous to many of his followers and Hugue's family is said to have received 107 lordships and manors, many of which were in Buckinghamshire and Oxfordshire. His Barony in Northumberland originally covered an extensive tract of land to the south of the River Tyne but, centuries later, the name of this small area of moorland is the only sign that it ever existed. The town of Bolbec, from which the family originally took its name, still exists lying just a few kilometers to the east of Le Havre in Normandy.

Pennypie House

3 As you approach the pumping station (surrounded by a mesh fence, stone wall and some pine trees), turn right at a finger post (signed 'Public Bridleway') to go around the corner of the pumping station to a gate. Through the gate, turn right through a pasture field, keeping a stone wall close by on your left.

4 Through a gate, follow a grass track that runs parallel with the stone wall over to your left. Gradually the track drifts away from this wall and then curves around to the right. Through another gate, turn half-left across the moor along a rushy path through the heather. The path skirts to the right of the grassy knoll of Birkside Fell with occasional waymarker posts helping to show you the route.

5 At the path junction, with the green fields of the valley of the Devil's Water in view ahead to the west, turn right: this is the Carrier's Way, an old pack horse trail used by lead miners in the 19th century (see Box C). After about 500 metres, go through a gate and carry on along the well trodden path over the brow of the hill. As the path crosses Bulbeck Common, there are other paths off to left and right, but keep straight ahead.

C During the 18th and 19th centuries, the hills and valleys of the North Pennines were at the centre of a thriving and prosperous lead mining industry. The mines were widely scattered across the landscape so the lead ore had to be transported by packhorse to one of the local smelt mills, such as at Rookhope in Weardale, Langley on the South Tyne or Dukesfield near Hexham. Over the centuries a network of packhorse routes was established across the hills with many acquiring a local name such as 'Black Way', 'Broad Way' 'Carrier's Way' and 'Long Drag'.

This section of the walk follows the 'Carrier's Way' which was used to transport lead ore from the mines in the East Allen Valley to the smelt mill at Dukesfield. The ore was carried by trains of between twelve and thirty 'Galloway' ponies, a small and sturdy breed that was well suited to the poor weather out on the fells and could comfortably carry a load of about 2 - 3 cwt. (100 - 150 kg), even along moorland tracks that became wet and boggy in the winter months. Evidence of the old packhorse trail can still be seen on this section of your walk as a wide shallow depression running along or parallel to the path.

Looking west over the valley of the Devil's Water from the Carrier's Way.

6 To the west of Warlaw Pike, go through a gate and continue along the path which passes close by some stone cairns as it heads towards the forest.

7 Through a gate at the moor edge, follow a track through a young broadleaved woodland (felled and replanted in about 2005), ignoring other forest tracks coming in from the left. Further on, the track heads into a conifer plantation.

Slaley Forest

[D] Most of Slaley Forest was planted in the 1950s and 1960s on land that would previously have been open moorland. To the right of the track, the first crop of trees, probably mostly pine and spruce, was felled in about 2005 and the land replanted with broadleaved species such as willow, birch and rowan. In the early years the young saplings are protected by tubular plastic guards which shelter them from the worst of the weather and prevent them being eaten by roe deer. To the left of the track the original crop was felled in about 1995 but here the land was replanted with Sitka spruce. This is a species from the Pacific coast of North America which thrives in the cool, damp climate and peaty soils of the British uplands, where it is now the most commonly planted tree. The Sitka spruce grows rapidly in these conditions and is usually felled at the age of about 40, when it will be converted into paper or chipboard or used to feed the growing demand for woodchips as a fuel for domestic heating systems. Sitka spruce can be distinguished from its close European relative, the Norway spruce (i.e. the Christmas tree) by the fact that the needles are sharper, a characteristic that is easily demonstrated by gently grasping the end of a branch.

8 At the fork in the track (i.e. stone track to the left and rough mud track to the right), bear left to go past a barrier and follow this track to a T-junction: here, turn left to get back to the start.

5. Spartylea and the Allen Valley

THE ALLEN VALLEY ONCE LAY AT THE HEART of the North Pennines lead mining industry and this walk starts out along 'The Black Way', an old pack horse trail that was used to transport lead ore across the moors from the mines at Nenthead. After dropping back down to the River East Allen near Spartylea, the return leg of the walk runs along the east side of the valley, with the final section across the heather moorlands of Sipton Law offering great views along the length of the dale.

OS Map: *1:25000 Explorer Maps OL43 (Hadrian's Wall) & OL31 (North Pennines)*
Start: *NY842510*
Grade: Strenuous, with the section across Sipton Law requiring careful navigation
Length: *5.3 miles (8.6 km) and about 3 hours*
Ascent: *305 metres (1000 feet), with some quite long and steep gradients*

Local services Allendale Village & Allenheads
Allendale Village & Allenheads
Spartylea, Allendale Village, Allenheads

From the centre of Allendale Town (where your should re-set your milometer trip), drive south along the B6295 towards Allenheads. After 3.5 miles, turn right down an unsigned road (there is an advance warning sign for the junction and the minor road itself has a 'Ford - 750 Yards' sign). This road winds its way down to the valley bottom where you should park in the small stone surfaced lay-by on the left side of the road, just before the ford across the River East Allen.

Cross the footbridge over the River East Allen and follow the road up the hill.

1 At the end of the tarmac road, keep straight on through a gate and along a stone track that heads uphill across the moor (signed 'Public Bridleway: Swinhope 1½; Coalcleugh 3½).

The Black Way close to High Knock Shield.

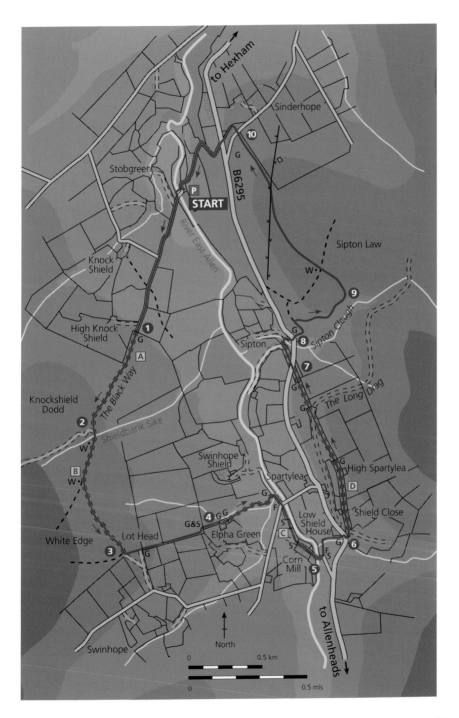

A The track along which you now walking is called 'The Black Way', one of a network of ancient pack horse routes across these wild uplands. During 18th and 19th centuries Allendale lay at heart of the North Pennines lead mining industry and teams of pack-horses were used to transport lead ore between the mines and the smelt mills, with the Black Way forming an important link between the mines at Nenthead (about 15 km to the south west) and the East Allen Valley. Later in your walk you will cross 'The Long Drag', another pack horse route that was used to take the ore onwards from Allendale to the Dukefield smelt mill on the Devil's Water, near Hexham (see Walk 2).

Not much is known about the hardy souls who earned their living as packhorse drivers – or 'jaggers' as they were sometimes known. They would certainly have had to be tough, crossing these moors in all weathers and able to defend themselves and their pack-trains from attack or robbery. Even today, the lives of these drivers can be witnessed in the names that they will have given to places along the way, such as Jagger Hill, Galloway Hill (the breed of horse favoured by the drivers) and Dead Horse Gulley (perhaps after a pack horse that didn't make it!).

2 At the track junction, bear left to go across Shieldbank Sike and continue past a waymarker post in a stone cairn. Over the brow of the next ridge keep straight on along the track, ignoring the waymarked public bridleway (the route of 'Isaac's Tea Trail'- see Box **B**) that heads off to the right over White Edge.

3 As the track passes close by the corner of a drystone wall, turn left off the track along an indistinct grass path, heading for an electricity pole about 20 metres to the right of the house at Lot Head. Go through a gate in the stone wall between the electricity pole and the house and walk down the field, keeping a fence and a broken-down stone wall close by on your right.

East across the Allen Valley from White Edge

B The path that heads to the right over Knockshield Moor is part of Isaac's Tea Trail (there is a special waymarker disc on the post) – this is a beautiful 36 mile circular walk through the heart of the North Pennines, starting and finishing at Isacc's Well in Allendale and passing through Sinderhope, Nenthead, Alston and Ninebanks. If you have the time and the energy it is a wonderful way of spending three or four days exploring some of the north of England's most stunning landscapes and was described in the Independent newspaper in 2010 as 'one of the last great undiscovered wilderness treks in England'.

Isaac's Tea Trail is named after an itinerant Victorian tea seller called Isaac Holden who started working in the Allendale lead mines at the tender age of 8 but, later in life, had to give this up when his health deteriorated and the mining industry went into decline. Isaac then embarked upon a new career as a travelling tea seller, with his wife running a grocers shop in Allendale. Over the years Isaac, dressed in black, became a familiar figure venturing out in all weathers selling tea door-to-door at farms and outlying villages. He is also remembered as a local fund raiser and his own account of his efforts to raise money for the purchase of a hearse provides a wonderful insight not only into his life but also that of village communities in rural Northumberland in the middle of the 19th century.

4 Go through a gate and into the yard beside Elpha Green. Keep to the left of the house to pass through a gate and on down the farm track. At the bottom of the track, turn right along a road. At the 3-way road junction beside Spartylea Bridge, go straight across to follow a grass path running in front of Tilery Cottage (signed 'Public Footpath: B6295 ½'). After going over three stiles this path brings you to the buildings at Corn Mill.

5 At the far end of the Mill, bear left across the bridge over the River East Allen; then, after 30 metres, turn left over a stone stile in the roadside wall and along a grass path (signed 'Public Footpath: Spartylea ½'): this soon brings you to a timber footbridge over the Ellershope Burn. 50 metres past the bridge, as the path comes out of the trees, turn right towards Low Shield House. Keep to the path along the right side of the stone wall around the house to reach a wicket gate onto the main road.

Wild thyme growing on rocks close to Tilery Cottage

[C] The mountain pansy (*Viola lutea*) must be one of the most beautiful flowers in the British Isles, with colours that vary from purple and mauve through to pale yellow and white. Fine black lines on the inner edges of the petals give each flower a distinctive 'pensive human face' - a characteristic that inspired its name, which is derived from the French word 'pensée' meaning 'thought'. From June through to August you will be able to see mountain pansies in the short grasslands along the banks of the River East Allen, with each colony tending to have a slightly different mix of colours.

Commercial varieties of garden pansy were developed in the early 19th century and are thought to be hybrids of the mountain pansy and the wild pansy (*Viola tricolor*), a flower that is quite common across lowland Britain on cultivated and waste ground and in short grassland. There are now many hundreds of different varieties of cultivated pansy but, to me, none seems to quite capture the delicacy and subtlety of the original.

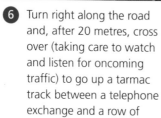

6 Turn right along the road and, after 20 metres, cross over (taking care to watch and listen for oncoming traffic) to go up a tarmac track between a telephone exchange and a row of cottages.

After a few metres, bear left to head uphill towards Shield Close. About ¼ mile past High Spartylea, go straight across a stone track (this is 'The Long Drag' - see Box [A]) and through a gate to continue along the grass path heading towards the cottages at Sipton.

7 Cross the main road (again taking care to watch and listen for oncoming traffic) and walk down the minor road opposite (signed 'Public Right of Way'). As this road bends left towards the cottages at Sipton, go right, along a rough track and across an old stone bridge. 50 metres past the bridge, turn sharp right back up to the main road.

8 Cross the road (again taking care!) and go through the gate opposite. Walk uphill along a grass path through the heather and after 70 metres follow the path sharp left. After another 100 metres, as the path forks, turn sharp right to follow a path that runs uphill alongside a shallow ditch with the valley of Sipton Cleugh over on your right.

9 After a few hundred metres the path curves left, away from Sipton Cleugh, and heads over the moor. At the brow of the hill and close to a waymarker post, go straight across another path (this is the bridleway to Sinderhope) and follow the path along the edge of the ridge, with views of the Allen Valley down to your left. Continuing along the ridge path you will see a line of electricity poles coming up from the left. Eventually, the path runs underneath the power line and becomes a wide grass track heading downhill with a stone wall close by on your right.

10 Go through the gate, then across the road towards a gate in a stone wall. In front of the gate, turn left along the wall and down to the main road. Cross the road (again taking care!), then walk down the minor road back to the start.

[D] One of Spartlea's most famous sons was the poet Barry MacSweeney who, although born in Newcastle, came from a Spartylea family and often visited his grandmother here. During the early 60's MacSweeney was one of the leading lights in the 'British Poetry Revival', a modernist inspired reaction against the more traditional and conservative styles of 20th century poetry. In 1967 MacSweeney and his colleagues organised the Spartylea Poetry Festival, a ten day session of reading, writing and discussion (and probably a fair bit of drinking) which succeeded in giving the 'Revival' the impetus it needed to effect a fundamental change in the direction of British poetry.

MacSweeney's poems have been described as 'sudden, terrifying and beautiful; darkly political, both extravagantly lyrical and harshly stripped back'. In the following lines from 'Pearl' (1995/7), he returns to his childhood memories of Spartylea:

> *Up a height or down the dale in mist or shine*
> *in heather or heifer-trampled marigold*
> *the curlew-broken silence sang its volumes.*
> *Leaning on the lichen on the Leadgate Road,*
> *Pearl said: a-a-a-a-, pointing with perfectly poised*
> *index finger towards the rusty coloured dry stone wall*
> *which contrasted so strongly with her milky skin.*

6. Staward Gorge and Plankey Mill

THE FIRST PART OF THIS WALK TAKES YOU THROUGH STAWARD GORGE, where the River Allen cuts through an impressive steep-sided valley that contains some of the most attractive and ecologically important woodlands in Tynedale. The half-way point at Plankey Mill, on the banks of the river, is a good spot for a picnic, before you climb out of the valley to return via Sillywrea Farm, one of the last farms in England to still use Clydesdale horses and where, on most days, you can see them working in the fields...or maybe having a well earned rest.

OS Map: *1:25000 Explorer Map OL43 Hadrian's Wall*
Start: *NY806596*
Grade: *Moderate but with some steep climbs and care required in places*
Length: *4.5 miles (7.8 km) and about 3 hours*
Ascent: *245 metres (800 feet) with some very steep ascents and descents*

Local services 🍵 Catton, Haydon Bridge & Allendale Town

🍺 Carts Bog, Catton, Allendale Town & Bearsbridge

🚌 Haydon Bridge & Allendale Town

Drive along the A686 (Haydon Bridge - Alston) to a point about ¾ mile west of the Carts Bog pub (which lies close to the junction with the B6305) and take the minor road heading south, signed to 'Allendale & Catton'. This road climbs up a gradient for about 100 metres then takes a sharp turn left over an old stone bridge. On the far side of the bridge, park on the wide grass verge on the right-hand side of the road - taking care not to block the gateway.

Walk back over the bridge and turn right, down to the main road. Cross the road (take care!) and go through the gate opposite (signed 'Public Footpath: Gingle Pot ½'). Follow the path that drops down to run close by a wood then continues over a stile to the old ruin of Gingle Pot.

The ruins at Gingle Pot - once a local inn

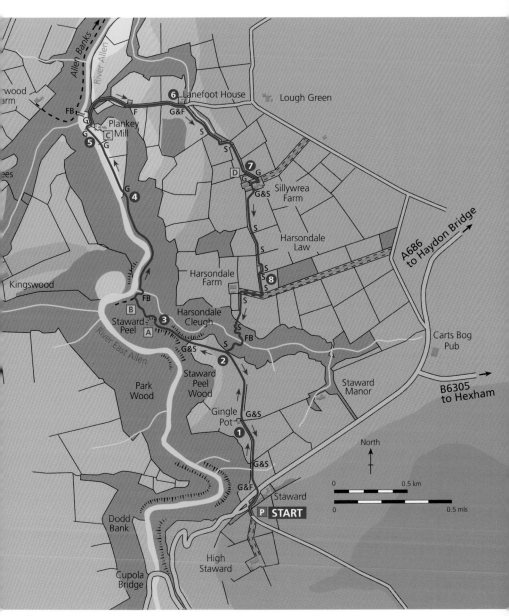

1 Go through a gate at Gingle Pot and continue along the brow of the hill, keeping a stone wall close by on your right.

2 Close to the wood at Harsondale Cleugh, take a path half-left across the field towards a gate in a stone wall. Go over a stile beside the gate to enter the National Trust's 'Staward Gorge' woodlands. The path runs along the top of a ridge with steep drops to either side – take care to stay away from the cliff edges and keep a watchful eye on any children or dogs.

3 On the west side of the ruins of Staward Peel (75 metres past an interpretation panel and the remains of the gatehouse), the path drops down to the right, close by a section of the old tower wall, then bends to the left to make a steep descent to the River East Allen. At the path T-junction in the valley bottom, turn right, then, about 50 metres further on, go right again to cross a timber footbridge. Follow the woodland path down-river for about ½ mile: again, please take care, there are some steep and precipitous drops down to the river off the left side of the path.

A From the 13th to the 16th century, the border lands between Scotland and England were a lawless place where 'reivers' looted and pillaged and life could be short and cheap. To protect themselves, those who had money built pele towers - like the one here at Staward: these were small fortified keeps where they could live in relative safety with their family and retainers, and offer local people a place of refuge when raiding parties swept across the border. Pele towers were primarily defensive and were built with thick stone walls, small windows and a single, small, heavy oak door. Reivers were lightly armed and attacked in small, mounted groups, relying on speed, surprise and mobility to capture livestock or to abduct people who could later be held to ransom. They were therefore not geared up for any kind of sustained siege so pele towers were an effective defence and, by having a beacon on their ramparts, the garrison could give warning to neighbouring settlements of any approaching danger.

© R.Johnson

Staward Gorge in autumn

B The descent down the valley side from Staward Peel to the River East Allen provides a graphic illustration of the difference between the ecology of broadleaved and conifer woodlands. At the top of the slope the path passes through a woodland of oak and birch in which the tree canopy admits sufficient light to allow the growth of a healthy ground flora characterised by species such woodrush, bilberry, heather and bracken (see photo right). There is also a scattering of seedlings and saplings which, in time, will grow up to fill any gaps in the canopy created by the death of older trees.

Further down the slope the character of the woodland changes completely as you enter the gloomy and lifeless world of a conifer plantation. Here the trees are mostly Western hemlock and Norway spruce, neither of which are native to the UK, with the hemlock originating in western North America and the spruce from continental Europe. The density of the canopy is such that virtually nothing can survive in the darkness below, other than occasional clumps of moss. The contrast is very stark and demonstrates why broadleaved woodlands are so much better for wildlife - and more pleasant for visitors.

© R.Johnson

4 At the end of the wood go through a wicket gate into a meadow and follow the riverside path towards Plankey Mill.

5 Near Plankey Mill, go through a gate close to the remains of the old footbridge parapet*, then turn right up the track towards the farm. Through another gate immediately in front of the old mill, turn left to follow the minor road heading uphill. (* If you want to extend your walk, you can continue downstream to Allen Banks by crossing the new footbridge over the River East Allen and turning right to follow the path along the west bank of the river.)

6 At Lanefoot House, turn right off the road through a wicket gate (signed 'Public Footpath: Sillywrea ½ Harsonside 1'), climb the short slope and keep to the path along the left edge of a field. Over two stiles and through two gates, you will come to a track at Sillywrea Farm.

41

Plankey Mill

The 'bench mark' at Plankey Mill

C Plankey Mill may look blissfully peaceful now but in past centuries it was part of a thriving farming and industrial community that stretched along the East Allen Valley. The origins of the Mill itself are unknown, although there is believed to have been a small farmstead here in the late 17th century and maps dating from the middle of the 19th century show the mill buildings together with a mill race which would have fed water from the nearby river to power the mill wheel. At this time it would have played a central role in the life of the community with local farmers bringing their wheat, barley and oats for grinding with the miller often receiving, in return, the 'miller's toll' of flour in lieu of his wages.

On the corner of the mill you can still see an old 'bench mark'. Long before the invention of GPS systems, bench marks were used by surveyors to accurately mark the location at which an elevation above sea level had been recorded; this could then be used as a reference point for other levelling surveys in the vicinity. Old Ordnance Survey maps used to record 'bench marks' with the acronym 'BM' followed by the elevation: this one is shown on the 1922 OS map as being at 330.7 feet which equals 100.8 metres if you want to check it against your (probably less accurate) GPS.

7 Turn right along the track then, immediately in front of the farmhouse gate, turn left between the farm buildings to go over a stile beside a gate. From here, walk up the slope ahead to cross a stone step-stile in the top right-hand corner of the field. Over four more stiles, and keeping to the right-hand side of the fields, continue over the top of Harsondale Law to the farm track leading to Harsondale Farm.

D Sillywrea is aptly named – it means 'Quiet Corner' and one thing that you can be sure you will not hear at Sillywrea is the throb of tractor engines because it is the only farm left in England using just horsepower. Sillywrea Farm covers about 200 acres of upland pasture and hayfields, with a small area set aside for arable crops such as mangel and turnip which are used to feed the cattle and sheep in winter. Most of the work done by the farm's horses therefore involves cutting, turning, baling and collecting the hay in early summer and then taking it back out into the fields in winter to feed the livestock - along with any other jobs that need a lot of muscle-power.

As you pass through the farm, you may see some of Sillywrea's six Clydesdale horses working in the fields or just having a well earned rest. Clydesdales are smaller than their larger cousins, the Shires, that one more often sees at county shows, but they are powerful, docile and very intelligent and, overall, are better suited to the type of work that they have to do on this upland farm. If you want to find out more about life at Sillywrea, a series of six half hour programmes called 'The Last Horsemen', together with an accompanying book, were produced in 2001 by Charles Bowden.

Hay cutting at Silly Wrea Farm

8 At the track, turn right towards the farm and, just before the farm gate, turn left over a ladder stile and walk down the field ahead, with an old hedge to your right. At the bottom of the field, go over a stile and (with care) follow the steep woodland path down to a footbridge over the Harsondale Burn. Climb up the other side of the valley to a stile in a fence: here, turn left along the path back to Gingle Pot and the start of the walk.

7. Hadrians Wall, Sewingshields and Broomlee Lough

STARTING FROM HOUSESTEADS, where you can take a close look at the impressive remains of a Roman Fort, this walk heads east along the line of Hadrian's Wall, with the summit of Sewingshields Crags offering spectacular views to the north and west. The loop back around Broomlee Lough takes you along some quiet paths and tracks to the north of the Wall and then along the route of the Pennine Way where the approach to Rapishaw Gap gives you a barbarian's eye view of this northern frontier to the Roman Empire.

OS Map: *1:25000 Explorer Map OL43 (Hadrian's Wall)*
Start: *NY794684*
Grade: Strenuous
Length: *6.6 miles (10.5 km) and about 4½ hours*
Ascent: *220 metres (720 feet), including a long climb up to Sewingshields Crags*

Local services 🚌 Housesteads, Haltwhistle & Hexham
🚍 Twice Brewed, Cawfields, Haydon Bridge, Bardon Mill
🚆 Haltwhistle & Hexham

Park in the National Trust Car Park at Housesteads: this is situated on the B6318 (Military Road) about 7 miles (12 km) west of Chollerford and 9 miles (14 km) east of Greenhead.

Go through the archway between the Visitor Centre and the Refreshments Kiosk, then turn left to a wicket gate and follow the stone track up towards Housesteads Fort.

1 Close to the Museum, where the track meets a tarmac road, bear slightly right to continue uphill across the grass, keeping close to the left-hand wall of the Fort and head towards the trees on the skyline.

If you want to have a closer look at the Fort, an entry ticket can be purchased at the Museum: this includes admission to the Museum's exhibition. Access around the outside of the Fort, including the route followed by this walk, is free of charge.

2 Close to the north-west corner of Housesteads Fort, go through a wicket gate, over Hadrian's Wall and down a few steps; then turn right to follow a path alongside the northern wall of the Fort (signed 'Hadrian's Wall Path: Sewingshields 2'). At the far end of the Fort, follow the Wall down into a shallow valley.

View towards Sewingshields Crags

A The Roman Empire lasted for over a thousand years and, at its peak in the early second century AD, it stretched from Britain to Egypt and covered an area of over 2 million square miles. When the Emperor Hadrian came to power in 117AD, the tribes of northern Britain had already been causing trouble so, rather than trying to conquer them, he opted for a more defensive strategy and (according to a contemporary biographer) decided 'to build a wall 80 miles long to separate the Romans from the barbarians'.

Hadrian's Wall stretched from Wallsend near Newcastle to Bowness on the Cumbrian coast and had a network of thirteen forts along its length, each about a day's march apart: Housesteads (or Vercovicius as the Romans called it) is the best preserved. Between adjacent forts they built milecastles and turrets to accommodate the soldiers that garrisoned each section of Wall. In front of the Wall, they constructed a defensive ditch, although along the high cliffs of the Whin Sill escarpment they didn't bother. Parallel to the Wall and set back at a distance of about 100 metres, they excavated the Vallum; an earthwork, comprising a ditch with mounds to either side, which is thought to have defined the southern boundary of the Wall's military zone. Sandwiched between the Wall and the Vallum was the Military Way, the Roman equivalent of a service road for troops and support staff. Many of these features are still visible along the section of Wall that you follow on this walk.

Housesteads Fort from the north east

3 At the bottom of the valley, go through a gate in a gap in the Wall, then turn sharp left up the hill (signed 'Hadrian's Wall Path: Sewingshields 1¾'), keeping Hadrian's Wall close by on your left. After about 50 metres, go over a stone step-stile in the field corner to follow a well defined path through a wood and then along the top of Kennel Crags.

4 Go past the stile and gate at King's Wicket and continue along the grass path by the wall, heading uphill to the summit of Sewingshields Crags and then on to Sewingshields Farm. Along the top of the Crags take great care – there are precipitous drops to your left.

B From Sewingshield's Crags the view west over Broomlee Lough and along the Whin Sill ridge is spectacular and gives a very tangible sense of the scale of Hadrian's Wall and of the landscape in which it was constructed.

Broomlee Lough (pronounced 'loff') is one of three lakes that have formed in the folds of land that lie to the north of the Wall. During the last Ice Age - about 25,000 years ago - this landscape was covered by immense glaciers which, as they moved slowly eastwards towards the sea, scoured away at the underlying rocks and shaped the landscape that we see today. As the glaciers retreated, the meltwaters collected in shallow depressions to form a series of loughs. Broomlee Lough is no more than about 10 feet deep and, at the more sheltered western end, reed beds and willow carr have developed to create a valuable habitat for wildlife. There is a legend that in the twelfth century a Dane called Oswald hid a treasure in the lough, casting a spell on it to prevent it being removed - except by twin horses, twin oxen, twin boys, and a chain forged by a seventh-generation blacksmith. Needless to say it has yet to be found or removed.

5 Close to Sewingshields Farm, go through a wicket gate and follow the path through the wood and around the north side of the farm buildings. 50 metres past the wicket gate on the far side of the wood, the path reaches a stone track close to small cottage: here, turn left and follow the track as it runs around the base of the wood and then heads north over a cattle grid.

6 Immediately over the next cattle grid, as the track bends sharp right, go half-left across a pasture field and head over a low ridge towards a broadleaved woodland on the far skyline. Over the brow of the ridge, keep just to the right of a small group of Scots pine where you will pick up a track heading west below the broadleaved woodland at King Wanless Green.

[C] Sewingshields Farm crouches in the lee of the Whin Sill, protected from the cold northerly winds by a dense plantation of sycamore trees - a species that was introduced to Britain from southern and central Europe by the Romans and which is one of the few broadleaved trees that is able to grow in this harsh and exposed landscape. Like many farms in this area, it was built from stone pillaged from the Wall at a time long before people were concerned about archaeological conservation or had given even a passing thought to its future tourism potential. Such a convenient and virtually unlimited supply of dressed stone was far too great a temptation to a poor hill farmer looking to build a house for himself and his family.

The name Sewingshields is derived from the old English for 'shiels of Sigewine', with a shiel being a small house or hut used by farmers during the summer months when their livestock was brought up from the lowlands to graze common land in the hills. In this part of Northumberland, the origins of many of the farms as a shiel can be traced in the frequent use of the word 'shield' in their present day name - such as Cawburn Shield, High Shield, Shield on the Wall, Low Old Shield and many more.

7 A couple of hundred metres past the end of the woodland, the track goes over a low ridge and then peters out. Continue in the same direction along the bottom of a shallow valley and make for a gate at the right-hand end of a stone wall about ¼ mile ahead.

8 Over the stile at Kingscrag Gate, keep to the path bearing slightly right. After about 150 metres this comes to a T-junction with a wide stone track: here, turn left and walk along the track as it heads south west. Half a mile further on, the track goes through a gate to continue in the same direction with Greenlee Lough coming into view ahead.

D About ¼ mile to the east of Sewingshields lies the flat expanse of Fozy Moss, one of the few examples of an intact upland peat bog that still exists in this part of Northumberland. In the Middle Ages most of these rolling uplands to the north of the Wall would have looked like this: wet, boggy, treeless and potentially treacherous…which is why the Border Reivers who roamed these hills were sometimes called 'Moss Troopers'. In the 19th and 20th centuries the economic pressures to make better use of these vast uplands meant that many of these mosses were planted with conifer trees or were drained and fertilized to improve the quality of the grazing for livestock. Nowadays only a few of the original mosses survive and these have become increasingly important, at a national and international level, as examples of a very rare and threatened wetland habitat.

9 At the junction with the route of the Pennine Way, close by some old stone sheep pens, turn left through a kissing gate to follow the Pennine Way heading south. Across Ridley Common the path crosses two ladder stiles before a steep climb up to Hadrian's Wall at Rapishaw Gap.

10 At Rapishaw Gap, go over a stile in a stone wall and turn sharp left to another stile: over this stile follow the path as it bends around to the right below a rocky outcrop. Walk along the base of the rocks for about 50 metres, then turn back sharp left up the slope to reach a path running alongside Hadrian's Wall.

11 Go through the gate and follow the path through the wood. At the end of the wood, turn right through a wicket gate and retrace your steps along the west side of Housesteads Fort and back to the car park.

Hadrian's Wall from Cuddy's Crags

8. Bellister Woods and along the Park Burn

THE BLUEBELLS THAT CARPET THE BELLISTER WOODLANDS in late April and early May are stunning - so save this walk for a spring day when the sun is shining. The first part of the walk follows a fairly level (but often muddy) path through the woods before passing the ruins of Bellister Castle and then heading south over the open moorlands of Broomhouse Common to the Park Burn: if you have brought a picnic, this is an ideal spot and it even has pretty waterfall nearby. The final section of the walk follows easy paths and tracks along the Park Burn and through Park Village.

OS Map: *Explorer Map OL43 (Hadrian's Wall)*
Start: *NY684620*
Grade: *Strenous, with some difficult conditions underfoot and tricky navigation*
Length: *4.3 miles (7.0 km) and about 3 hours*
Ascent: *120 metres (400 feet)*

Local services   Haltwhisltle

Featherstone Rowfoot & Haltwhisltle

Haltwhistle

Turn off the Haltwhistle bypass along the road heading south to 'Alston, Halton-lea-Gate and Coanwood'. Drive along here for just over a mile, then turn right along the minor road signed to 'Kellah'. After another ¼ mile and just past the entrance to the Haltwhistle Camping and Caravan Club site, park in the lay-by on the left, beside the parapet of the old stone bridge over the Park Burn.

Please Note: The section over Broomhouse Common can be quite difficult so go prepared with appropriate footwear and clothing: it also requires some careful navigation so please pay close attention to the route description and map.

To start the walk, head back up the road for about 50 metres and turn left through a wicket gate into the woodlands of the National Trust's Bellister Estate. Keep along the main path through the wood, ignoring any side paths to left and right.

Early purple orchids in a roadside verge near Bellister

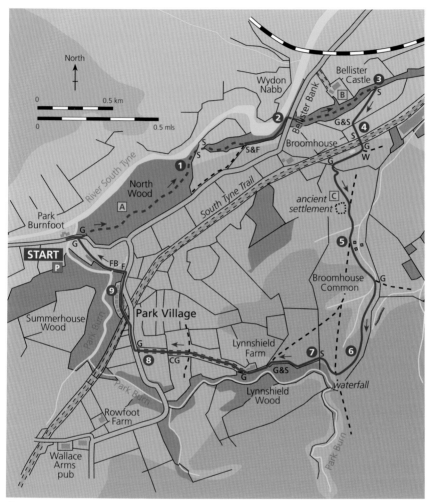

1 At the end of the wood, go over a stile in a fence and, following the contour, walk a few metres to go over a ladder-stile into another woodland. The path soon climbs up to run along the top edge of the wood and past a path heading back to Park Village.

2 Close to the road at Bellister Bank, the path forks: here, bear left downhill for about 100 metres to go through a gap in the roadside fence. Taking care to watch and listen for traffic, cross the road to a gap in a fence on the far side and continue along the path through the woodland. Bellister Castle soon comes into view through the trees on your left

A In early May the woods at Bellister are carpeted with bluebells and it is an ideal time to enjoy nature at its very best. The bluebell is most commonly found in broadleaved woodland and, along with species such as dog's mercury, wild garlic and wood anemone, is one of a small group of plants known as 'woodland indicators', which tend to be found only on land that has been covered in woodland for much of the last 5000 years. Whilst the presence of these species suggests that this is likely to be the case here at Bellister, the character of the woodland has probably changed a great deal as a result of management for timber production and the introduction of non-native species such as sycamore. Across the British Isles there are now few, if any, genuinely natural remnants of the 'primary woodland' that became established across much of the lowlands after the last Ice Age. Many of these woods had been lost even by Elizabethan times and, more recently, the final nail in the coffin was the massive demand for timber arising from the industrial revolution and two World Wars.

3 Shortly after reaching a fence along the top edge of the wood, climb over a stile and cut back half-right across a field, heading over the brow of a low ridge. At a stone wall, go over a step-stile beside a gate and head straight across a field to drop down towards the disused railway line that now forms the South Tyne Trail.

Bellister Castle

B From the path you can only see a part of Bellister Castle, most of which dates from the 19th and early 20th centuries when it was extensively rebuilt. Alongside this, and mostly hidden from view, are the ruins of a much earlier fortified 'hall house' which may date from the 13th or 14th centuries when this border country was a lawless place. Protection from bands of reivers was fairly essential if, like the Blenkinsopps who built it, you had money and wanted to keep it…and your life.

Like any self respecting castle, Bellister has its resident ghost. Legend has it that centuries ago a wandering minstrel was turned out of the castle on suspicion of being a spy and was afterwards hunted down by the Lord's pack of blood hounds. He met an unpleasant death somewhere near the river and his ghost, the Grey Man of Bellister, has stalked the castle ever since. Whilst on this grisly theme, the castle grounds also have an old sycamore tree, known as The Hanging Tree, where, during the English Civil War, royalist cavaliers are reputed to have hung defeated Parliamentary troops.

4 Go over an old concrete stile, then across the Trail and through a gate on the far side. After about 50 metres the path forks: take the right fork along a grass track that runs gradually uphill (signed on a waymarker post as a 'public bridleway') towards a dry stone wall. Go through a gate in the wall and turn left along a track that winds uphill onto the moor.

The River South Tyne and Haltwhistle

C On the moorland to the right of the path there are the remains of an old settlement that probably dates from the mediaeval period - usually defined as the time between the Norman invasion of 1066 and the Union of the Crowns in 1603. The only visible evidence of its existence are a few humps and hollows where the houses would have stood, with the faint line of an embankment and ditch tracing the boundary of a rectangular enclosure around the settlement that may have offered some limited defence or been used to control livestock.

Small settlements such as this one would probably have been occupied by an extended family of peasant farmers who worked the surrounding land. At this time there were various types of peasants known by titles such as cottars, bordars, bondmen, villeins, neyfs and serfs, some of whom were free to work their own land whilst others were effectively the property of the local lord, with no freedom to work for themselves. Social mobility was not high on the political agenda of mediaeval feudal society and it was difficult, if not impossible, for individuals to move up the ladder from one social class to another.

5 About 150 metres past a stream the path forks: here, bear left to follow a grass path (past some small fenced tree enclosures) that runs along the top edge of the ridge above the shallow valley on your left. Follow this path south across Broomhouse Common, keeping roughly parallel to the stone wall about 50 -100 metres to your left. At times this path becomes indistinct but you will not lose your way if you keep the stone wall in view on your left.

6 As the woodlands along the Park Burn come into view over to your right, bear right and head towards them. At the edge of the ravine, turn right* along a path to a ladder stile over a stone wall. (* If you have the time, it is worth making a short detour by turning left here to see a pretty little waterfall down in the valley below - and its a nice place for a picnic if you have brought one.)

7 Over the stile walk beside the woodland fence towards Lynnshield Farm. Close to the farm, go through a wicket gate then along the edge of a deep wooded ravine, to pass just to the left of the farmhouse and barns. At the end of the barns go through a wicket gate and turn left along the farm access track.

8 Cross the road (taking care to watch and listen for oncoming traffic) and turn right to walk along the grass verge. After about 150 metres bear left along the side-road through Park Village.

9 On reaching the main road on the far side of the village, turn left and walk along the roadside verge: after 100 metres take the path left (signed 'Public Footpath: Burnfoot ¼') down a few steps to a timber footbridge. Over the bridge the path keeps close to a woodland fence on your left. It then drops down to cross a pasture and heads for a wicket gate at the end of the old stone bridge over the Park Burn where you parked your car.

Looking east from Broomhouse Common

9. Featherstone, Lambley and the South Tyne Trail

ALTHOUGH IT IS JUST UNDER 5 MILES IN LENGTH, this is a reasonably easy walk since it has few climbs, is easy to navigate and there are usually good conditions underfoot: a great walk for a winter's day, with a country pub at the end to warm you up and revive the spirits. The outward leg along the banks of the South Tyne and through the parklands around Featherstone Castle is delightful. A short climb then takes you up onto the South Tyne Trail, the former Haltwhistle - Alston railway, which takes you all the way back to the start and offers the opportunity for a short diversion to see the impressive Lambley Viaduct.

OS Map: *1:25000 Explorer Map OL43 (Hadrian's Wall)*
Start: *NY682608*
Grade: *Easy/Moderate*
Length: *4.8 miles (7.8 km) and about 3 hours*
Ascent: *60 metres (200 feet)*

Local services   ☕ Haltwhisltle

               🍴 Featherstone Rowfoot & Haltwhisltle

               🚌 Haltwhistle

Turn off the Haltwhistle bypass along a road heading south signed to 'Alston, Halton-lea-Gate and Coanwood'. After 2¼ miles, turn right (at a converted chapel) along a minor road signed to 'Featherstone Park'. The Wallace Arms pub soon appears on your left: 100 metres past the pub, turn left into the 'South Tyne Trail – Featherstone Park Station Car Park'.

From the car park, climb a few steps onto the South Tyne Trail (a walking/cycling route along the track-bed of the former Alston - Haltwhistle railway) and turn right to go through a gate and across a road, taking care to watch and listen for oncoming traffic. On the far side of the road, continue along the Trail (signed 'Public Footpath: Park Village ⅔'), passing beside the old station platform.

Walking the South Tyne Trail

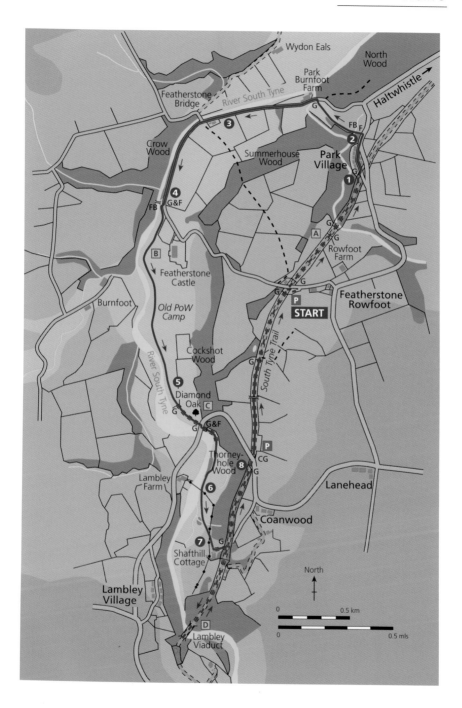

Wydon Eals

North Wood

Haltwhistle

Park Burnfoot Farm

Featherstone Bridge

River South Tyne

G

FB F

2

Crow Wood

3

Summerhouse Wood

Park Village

G

1

4

G&F

FB

G

A

G

Rowfoot Farm

B

Featherstone Castle

G

G

Featherstone Rowfoot

Burnfoot

Old PoW Camp

P

START

River South Tyne

Cockshot Wood

G

South Tyne Trail

5

Diamond Oak

C

G

G&F

G

Thorney-hole Wood

8

P

CG

G

Lanehead

Lambley Farm

6

Coanwood

7

G

Shafthill Cottage

North

Lambley Village

0   0.5 km

0   0.5 mls

D

Lambley Viaduct

57

A The South Tyne Trail is a walking and cycling route that runs for 23 miles from Haltwhistle in the Tyne Valley to Alston, high up in the North Pennines. The Trail was created in the early 1990s on the line of the former Alston – Haltwhistle railway, which was closed in 1976 as part of the 'reshaping of British railways' advocated by the 1963 Beeching Plan.

The origins of the railway line go back to the 18th century when the North Pennines lay at the centre of a thriving lead mining industry. In the early days, the lead was transported by pack horses and horse-drawn wagons but the expansion of the railway network westwards along the Tyne Valley offered the opportunity to bring a new branch line into the heart of the North Pennine lead mining communities. The Haltwhistle to Alston line was opened in 1852 and included the impressive Lambley Viaduct over the South Tyne, a masterpiece of Victorian engineering that is still standing and is well worth a visit (see Box **D**). The creation of this railway was not only vital to the lead mining industry but also encouraged the extraction of other ores and minerals such as iron, coal, fluospar and limestone and helped in the development of Tyneside as a major industrial centre. By the early years of the 20th century, the gradual closure of the lead mines and collieries had sounded the death knell for the railway and, although it struggled on with freight and passenger traffic until the 1970s, its eventual closure became inevitable.

1 Close to Park Village and just before a stone bridge over the Trail, take a small path to the left to climb a gentle slope. At the top, go through a wicket gate and turn left along the road through the village.

2 On reaching the main road, turn left and walk along the roadside verge. After 100 metres take the path left (signed 'Public Footpath: Burnfoot ¼') down a few steps to a timber footbridge. Over the bridge the path keeps close to a woodland fence on your left and then drops down to cross a pasture and heads for a wicket gate at the end of an old stone bridge over the Park Burn. Through the gate, turn left past Park Burnfoot Farm and walk along the roadside verge beside the River South Tyne.

3 Continue along the road past Featherstone Bridge.

4 Close to the footbridge over the South Tyne, turn right off the road to go through a wicket gate, then take an immediate left (signed 'Public Bridleway 300 yds then Public Footpath Diamond Oak 1') to head upstream along the riverside path. Continue along this path for the next mile but take great care to keep away from the river bank which is seriously eroded and in many places is under-cut.

Featherstone Castle

B The first known reference to Featherstone Castle dates from the 13th century when it is described as a Manor in the Barony of Langley in the ownership of Helias de Featherstonehaugh. The original castle dates from this period and was relatively unscathed by the centuries of border feuding that followed. The Union of the Crowns in 1603 ushered in a period of relative peace and the castle was gradually restored and extended to create the building that you see today.

As you walk along the river you will also see the remains of a prisoner of war camp dating from World War II. It was initially built as a training camp for American troops but between 1945 and 1948 it housed some 25,000 Italian and German prisoners. The camp was widely regarded as being one of the most effective rehabilitation camps in the country and became known as the 'camp of confidence'. On the gate post at the entrance there is a plaque commemorating Captain Sulzbach, the camp interpreter from 1946, who was central to the camp's success in promoting Anglo-German friendship in the post-war years.

Left: Featherstone Bridge was constructed in 1775 to allow lead ore from the mines up-river to be transported over the River South Tyne to the smelting mill at Haltwhistle. The bridge has a rather lop-sided appearance because the keystone on the main arch is off-centre from the apex of the parapet.

5 Below Cockshot Wood, go through a gate in a fence line: the Diamond Oak is over to your left (see Box C). The next gate takes you onto a road close to a new bridge over the South Tyne: here, turn right for 25 metres, then cross the road (take care!) and head along a track through a gate (signed 'Public Footpath: Coanwood ¾'). After a couple of hundred metres the track peters out but keep heading south with the riverbank to your right.

6 As you pass under an overhead power line, bear slightly left away from the river, following a faint grass path that keeps to the right of the power line. After skirting to the left of a small copse of alder trees, the path passes under the power line and heads towards Shafthill Cottage.

Erosion on the River South Tyne at Featherstone

C Just to the left of the path you will see the 'Diamond Oak', a famous old oak tree that is even named on Ordnance Survey maps of the area. No-one seems to know how it got its name but it must have had it for a long time because it even appears on a map dating from 1862. The most likely reason is that it was planted to commemorate the diamond jubilee of some historic event, although its large size suggests that this would have been a very long time ago.

In the UK oaks grow to a greater age than most other species of tree and researchers working in the oak forests of The Weald in Kent have developed a method of calculating the age of ancient oak trees according to their circumference at a height of 1.5 metres. The Diamond Oak is 6.2 metres in circumference, which equates to an age of about 430 years, taking us back to the reign of Queen Elizabeth I during the late 16th century.

Right: Lambley Viaduct from the north

7 At the cottage, turn left and climb a steep stone track. Go through a gate at the top of the hill and follow the track immediately on your left that runs alongside the old platform of Coanwood Station. If you want to see the Lambley Viaduct - an impressive 19th century railway bridge across the River South Tyne - you will need to a make a detour of about ¼ mile (each way) along the Trail to the right.

8 At the northern end of Thorneyhole Wood, go through a gate and across a road to continue through a car park and along the South Tyne Trail (signed 'Public Footpath: Featherstone Rowfoot 1'). This takes you back to the car park at Featherstone Rowfoot. If you have worked up a thirst or feel hungry, the Wallace Arms is usually open most of the day and serves real ales and pub lunches.

D The Lambley Viaduct is one of those wonderfully impressive Victorian structures that characterise the 'no problem is too big' philosophy of 19th century engineers. It opened in 1852 and formed the final link in the Haltwhistle - Alston railway which had been built to haul coal and lead from the North Pennines down to the Tyne Valley and on to Newcastle. The designer was a young engineer from Newcastle called George Barclay-Bruce who had been an apprentice to Robert Stephenson and went on to build railways across the world, including the Royal Border Bridge across the River Tweed at Berwick; a bridge that, to this day, carries the East Coast Main Line.

After the closure of the line in 1976 the viaduct started to deteriorate, with trees and shrubs growing out of cracks in the masonry and chunks falling off into the valley below. Fortunately, in 1991 the British Rail Property Board agreed to repair the viaduct and hand it over to the North Pennines Heritage Trust who allow visitors to walk across, although the track is blocked at the western end because the old Lambley Station is now a private house.

10. Knarsdale and the South Tyne Valley

A GOOD WALK FOR A WINTER'S DAY with not too much climbing, good conditions underfoot and a pub along the way (open lunchtimes Wed – Sun). After a short section along the road from Slaggyford Village, the walk follows an ancient cart track along the flanks of Williamston Common with lovely views along the South Tyne Valley. Crossing the river by the old stone bridge at Eals, the final section makes for easy going along quiet country lanes and the South Tyne Trail, a walking route on the line of a former railway line.

OS Map: *1:25000 Explorer Map (OL43 Hadrian's Wall)*
Start: *NY677524*
Grade: *Strenous*
Length: *5.3 miles (8.6 km) and about 3 hours*
Ascent: *140 metres (460 feet)*

Local services 🚌 Alston & Haltwhistle

🅟 Knarsdale, Featherstone Rowfoot, Alston & Haltwhistle

🚮 Alston & Haltwhistle

Turn off the Haltwhistle bypass along a road heading south signed to 'Alston, Halton-lea-Gate and Coanwood'. After about 5 miles this brings you to a T- junction with the A689: here, turn left and head towards Alston. After a further 5 miles, at the village of Slaggyford, turn right and park on the side of the road close to the village green.

Walk back down to the main road and turn right. Please take great care on this section along the main road: keep to the verge wherever possible, walk in single file, and watch and listen for oncoming traffic.

1 After about 500 metres, turn left along a minor road signed to Barhaugh Hall. Go across the bridge over the South Tyne and follow the road around a couple of bends, then turn left along a track to Williamston (signed 'Public Footpath: Parson Shield 1; The Bog 2'). Follow the track to the left around the back of the cream-painted farmhouse, then through a gate and bear right to head uphill onto the fell.

Wych elm seeds. Following the loss of millions of elms through Dutch Elm Disease, the wych elm is now quite a rare tree but can still be found along the River South Tyne

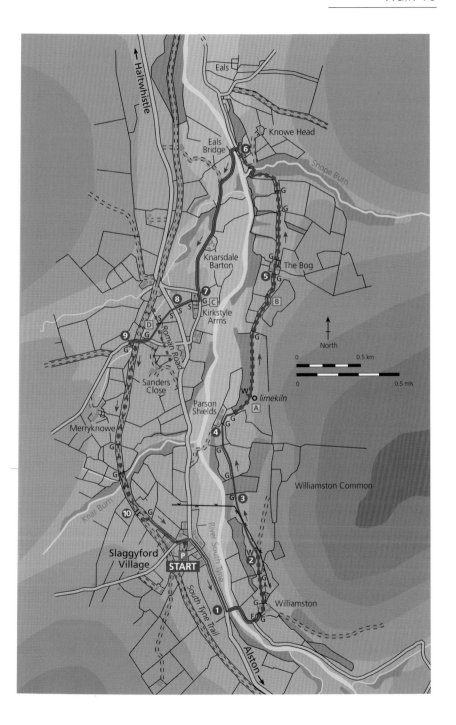

2 About 20 metres before the track passes underneath an electricity line, turn left at a waymarker post and follow the path that runs along the contour, with the South Tyne below and to your left.

3 Go through the gates on either side of a young plantation, then across a pasture field with a fence close by on your left. Through another gate the path leads on to the farm at Parson Shields.

4 Just before the gate into the farmyard at Parson Shields, go right, through another gate that takes you alongside a stone wall. About 50 metres through this gate and just past the end of the first of two large barns, turn sharp right to head uphill over a small stream to a gate in a stone wall. Through the gate, continue uphill along a track. Close to an old lime kiln the track bears left at a waymarker post to follow the contour northwards along the hillside.

A The old lime kiln on the right-hand side of the path dates from the 19th century and was built to convert limestone taken from a nearby quarry into quicklime for use in farming and building. This process involved tipping limestone and coal into the conical chamber or 'pot' at the top of the kiln and then burning the mixture for several hours. This converted the limestone into quicklime which could then be shovelled from the small brick-arched opening at the base of the kiln, before being loaded onto wagons and carted away. After being slaked with water it was then spread on pastures to sweeten the soil and improve the grass.

Although the kiln is quite well preserved, the back of the pot has started to collapse so please be careful. If you walk on along the track for a few yards and then cut back to the right you will be able to see the top of the pot (now with an ash tree growing out of it) and the remains of the old limestone quarry cut into the hillside behind. The track along which you are walking will also have been used to cart coal to the kiln from local mines and to transport the quicklime out to farms in the area.

B The hillside to the right of the track is covered in juniper scrub and, as one of the most important examples of its kind in Northumberland, has been declared a Site of Special Scientific Interest by Natural England. Juniper is one of only three native conifer species in the British Isles - the others are yew and Scots pine - and it is certainly the rarest with its greatest claim to fame being that its berries are used as the main flavouring in gin production.

Due to their exposed location the juniper bushes scattered along this hillside look small and scrubby but most are believed to between 70 and 120 years old. Unfortunately, juniper doesn't naturally regenerate very well so Natural England and the farmer have given it a helping hand by growing young trees from seed collected locally and then transplanting these back onto the hill, using plastic tubes to give them a bit of shelter and keep off hungry rabbits. This technique looks as though it is having some success and should help to conserve this valuable habitat, although it is a very long term project because juniper grows so slowly.

Left: The hillside track heading north from the old lime kiln

5 At The Bog farm, go through the gates into the farmyard, then bear left between the buildings to go through a couple more gates and along the tarmac track continuing north. This track leads to a wooded valley and a bridge over the Snope Burn; 50 metres past the bridge, be sure to take the track straight ahead (ignoring the track right to Knowe Head).

6 Turn left over Eals Bridge and follow the road past Knarsdale Barton.

7 Just past the road junction, you will find the Kirkstyle Inn, a country pub that can offer a welcome pint and other refreshments. The route of our walk goes through the metal gate of the church (signed 'Public Footpath') and across the graveyard. Over the stile on the far side, head across the field keeping a stone wall close by on your right, to reach a stone step-stile in the field corner.

[C] The present Church of St Jude dates from 1833, although this replaced an earlier building which a drawing shows to have been in ruins in 1810; the sundial on the south wall is probably the only remnant. Originally the church had no dedication and it was only in 1968 that it was put under St. Jude's patronage. St Jude, or Thaddeus as he is sometimes known, is one of the lesser known of the twelve apostles and is not to be confused with Judas Iscariot who betrayed Jesus for 30 pieces of silver. In the Roman Catholic church he is the patron saint of desperate cases and lost causes.

Almost next door to the church is the Kirkstyle Inn, a pleasant little country pub that serves real ales and bar lunches. It is certainly in an out-of-the-way location with no other pubs for several miles in either direction: this is believed to have been because years ago the local landowner was a rabid teetotaller and would not permit the sale of alcohol.

The South Tyne Valley near Knarsdale Barton

8 Cross the main road (take care – traffic travels fast along this section) then over the stile on the far side (signed 'Public Footpath'): from here, bear slightly left towards the highest point of the stone wall on the far side of the field to reach a stone step-stile a few metres to the left of the field corner. Continue in the same direction across the next field to go through a gate close to the right-hand end of a small conifer plantation and turn right along a road.

D The stile in the field corner lies very close to the route of an old Roman Road which, when the sun is low in the sky, can still be seen as a very faint line in the grass either here or just to the south of the road ahead (see the map for an indication of its route). The road is called 'The Maiden Way' and connected Hadrian's Wall (at the 'Magnis' Roman fort at Carvoran near Greenhead) with the arterial Roman Road between York and Penrith (meeting it at 'Bravoniacum' Roman fort at Kirby Thore, near Appleby).

During their four centuries of occupation, the Romans constructed a network of some 2000 miles of paved roads which enabled them to move troops and military equipment rapidly across the country and encouraged trade and the easy flow of goods. As one of the principal links to the empire's northern border at Hadrian's Wall, the Maiden Way would have been vital for the movement of men, equipment and food, especially at times when the northern tribes were revolting against Roman rule. Such roads would have remained in use for centuries after the Romans left Britain in the early 5th century and, even today, some of our main roads have been built on the same line, with their straightness often being a tell-tale sign of their Roman origins.

9 About 50 metres past the bridge over the track-bed of the old railway line (now the South Tyne Trail), turn left through the left-hand of a pair of gates to cross a small patch of boggy ground down to a wicket gate, then turn right along the South Tyne Trail.

10 The South Tyne Trail continues south over the Knar Burn Viaduct and then under an old stone-arched bridge. About 75 metres past this bridge, turn left then immediately right through a gate and along a path leading back to the village green at Slaggyford.

The South Tyne Valley to the south of Slaggyford